Artist, fighter – and friend

Robin Page

Country Diary

I WILL always remember May 4, 1998. It was the day after my birthday; the sun was warm, bringing out the first orange-tip butterfly of the year and the apple blossom in my garden was at its peak. On the Countryside Restoration Trust land a thousand cowslips bloomed and, above, larks sang. There was a beautiful fusion of scents, sounds and sights; it was the art of nature.

Such a day required a painting; a painting of a day that was quintessentially English. There was only one man who could have caught the mood to perfection — but tragically this was the day my friend Gordon Beningfield died.

There is always sadness after an illness bravely fought, but with Gordon the sense of loss has been intensified by the season of his going. He loved the spring and only 10 days earlier he had said from his hospital bed: "This is my favourite time of the year — what a time to be in here." The legacy of paintings he leaves behind shows his love of the English spring — bluebell woods with fallow deer, "windflowers", butterflies and an appreciation that made him the outstanding countryside painter of his generation.

How I will miss him; as a friend, a confidant, my hoped-for Best Man and as vice-chairman of the CRT. It was at this time of year that the phone calls would come thick and fast. "I've seen my first swallow . . . my first swift . . . my first orange tip . . ." His enthusiasm never faded and each year there would be new finds, new experiences, visits to Hardy country, rides on steam trains, visits to this field, and even journeys to Duxford to see his favourite man-made bird, the Spitfire. In the background, always, was Betty, his childhood sweetheart turned wife — companion, friend and certainly the best country cook in Hertfordshire.

We were friends from the instant we met, well over 20 years ago. He came to interview me about my tame vixen for a television programme. We had much in common; we were both uneducated innocents in a very competitive and predominantly urban world — he with his paintbrush, me with my pen.

Our interests were almost identical except for one thing — I was embarrassingly ignorant about butterflies. Gordon was a self-taught expert whose expertise showed itself in his paintings, as he transformed butterfly "illustration" into genuine art. His enthusiasm pulled me into the world of butterflies: "There's an orange-tip. Let's look for its eggs on the cuckoo flower" — and there they were.

His enthusiasm gave rise to anger as he saw the countryside being ruined by intensive farming and the CAP, thanks in his view to Edward Heath "the traitor", or "the bloater", according to his mood. Each ripped-out hedgerow, ruined badger sett and felled tree he felt personally, a loss that depressed him and made him even more determined to fight the advance of the evil agricultural and planning empires.

It was in 1980 that he decided we should enlist the help of the RSPB, and we rushed off to Sandy to demand that the then director, Ian Prestt, make a stand for the countryside as a whole and not just special reserves. It was a memorable meeting — one that had Gordon banging the table in frustration to emphasise his point, something that does not happen to the head of the RSPB every day.

But although he felt the destruction of the countryside deeply, he could also be a very happy and funny man. Each year we would visit the Shire Horse Show at Peterborough and somehow he always got into the Press tent for a bacon sandwich breakfast. Then there was the Game Fair: Gordon the perfect gentleman, immaculate in his John Brocklehurst country clothes; me the ragged peasant, shambolic in my trainers and jeans.

I shared many public platforms with him over the years when he spoke with passion and humour with not a note in sight. The halls were almost always packed for he had the common touch and people of all ages were attracted to him and loved him.

As we saw the countryside being steadily eroded, the idea of the Countryside Restoration Trust gradually formed and he had no hesitation in becoming a trustee — travelling to all the meetings, open days and December barn dances.

When his illness returned it was hard. He desperately wanted to produce another book — *Beningfield's Vanishing Song Birds* — and he completed some stunning new paintings. He hated missing the Countryside March in the spring: he did not hunt, he stopped shooting and his trout river dried up, but he believed that hunting and all the other countryside issues — the CAP, the Green Belt, the closure of village schools, the power of the supermarkets and the rest — were worth marching for.

Strangely, as I write this piece and another orange tip flutters through my garden, I do not feel desolate. Instead, I simply feel honoured to have had such a friend and determined to continue the fight for the countryside he loved so much. Part of that determination, I hope, will lead to the CRT getting a farm in Dorset. Then a little part of Hardy Country will become Beningfield Country. It will be a fitting tribute to a sensitive, gifted, good man.

● *A memorial service for Gordon Beningfield will be held in St Albans Abbey on Friday, May 29, at 2pm.*

Picture: ALAN SOUTHGATE

'We were uneducated innocents in a very competitive world'

Hardy countryman: Gordon in Dorset

BENINGFIELD'S BUTTERFLIES

Beningfield's BUTTERFLIES

Paintings and Drawings by
GORDON BENINGFIELD

Text by
ROBERT GOODDEN

VIKING

VIKING
Penguin Books Ltd, Harmondsworth, Middlesex, England
Viking Penguin Inc., 40 West 23rd Street, New York, New York 10010, U.S.A.
Penguin Books Australia Ltd, Ringwood, Victoria, Australia
Penguin Books Canada Limited, 2801 John Street, Markham, Ontario, Canada L3R 1B4
Penguin Books (N.Z.) Ltd, 182-190 Wairau Road, Auckland 10, New Zealand

First published by Chatto & Windus, 1978
Second edition published by Chatto & Windus and by Penguin Books, 1981
Published by Viking, 1986

This edition produced by Cameron Books, 2a Roman Way, London N7 8XG

Edited and designed by Ian Cameron

Printed in Holland by de Lange/van Leer b.v., Deventer
Bound in England by R.J. Acford, Chichester, Sussex

British Library Cataloguing in Publication Data available

CONTENTS

The four new pictures which appear in this edition of *Beningfield's Butterflies* were painted in Spring 1980 as designs for a set of stamps commissioned by the British Post Office for issue on 13th May 1981. They are reproduced at their original size. The subjects are the Peacock (frontispiece), Chequered Skipper (p.6), Large Blue (p.11) and Small Tortoiseshell (p.15). They are reproduced by kind permission of the Post Office.

INTRODUCTION

The seventy or so British butterflies represent six families. The Browns of the Satyridae and the Skippers of the Hesperiidae are grassland butterflies. The Pieridae include the Whites of woodland and garden as well as the migrant Clouded Yellow. The Blues and Coppers of the downlands and the Hairstreaks from the woodlands belong to the Lycaenidae. The largest family, the Nymphalidae, includes Fritillaries, Emperors, Admirals and a group of Vanessids such as the Peacock and Painted Lady. Two butterflies are the sole British representatives of their families, the Swallowtail (Papilionidae) and the Duke of Burgundy Fritillary (Nemeobiidae).

Although lepidopterists may know when and where to look for almost any butterfly and may well be able to find it, subjective opinions that there are less butterflies around than there were even a few years ago certainly have a basis in fact. The unusual abundance of the commoner species in a warm year like 1976 may temporarily veil the fact that some species are now found in only half the localities where they could be seen in the 'fifties.

The Large Blue occurred in thousands well into the 'sixties, but it was down to less than fifty butterflies when the first edition of this book appeared in 1978. Before Gordon Beningfield had completed the originals for the Post Office's butterfly stamps, the Large Blue was declared extinct in Britain. While its decline was closely monitored, the Chequered Skipper has slipped quietly away: in less than a decade, the population south of the Scottish border has gone from thousands to zero. It is saved from extinction only by its survival in a single Scottish locality which was discovered as recently as 1942. Even such migrants as the Clouded Yellow have not been seen recently in the quantities that were once considered usual.

The complex of factors behind the decline is not fully understood. Climate greatly influences the fluctuation in numbers, producing increases in good summers. Mild, damp winters affect the hibernating stages and tend to result in fewer butterflies than cold ones, when hibernation is deep and undisturbed.

Climate is the one factor that we cannot influence, but other causes of the decline of butterflies and wildlife in general are to a large extent in our hands. The introduction of agricultural insecticides is popularly accepted as the main cause for the disappearance of butterflies. At most, insecticides are only part of the problem. They are less significant than the continued destruction of the wild countryside that stems from human pressures. Simply condemning development is naive; towns and roads have to be built and agriculture requires land. Between ardent conservationists and all except the most blinkered planners there can be mutual understanding and valid compromise. The Forestry Commission, which is sometimes criticised for its necessarily commercial policy of planting coniferous forest, now encourages the growth of vegetation that is necessary for butterflies, birds and other wildlife. The Commission is often very co-operative in allowing naturalists to make detailed studies on its land. The divergent aims of planners and conservationists have on occasion been satisfactorily resolved by changing the site of building works or diverting intended roads. But the outcome cannot always be successful for both sides. The important thing is for people to be aware of the importance of conservation: much of conservationists' work is a matter of education.

The County Naturalists' Trusts do much to promote conservation and carry out valuable practical work. With the help of people who want to do something towards halting the decrease in the number of butterflies, the British Butterfly Conservation Society (Tudor House, Quorn, Leicestershire) is running the countrywide Habitat Survey Scheme to study the ecological factors involved in numerical fluctuations. The principal aim is to establish ways in which the decline can be stemmed and in which wastage can be prevented when stock is introduced to augment wild populations.

Even within the confines of a garden, much can be done to encourage butterflies and contribute to their survival. They need a great deal of nectar; only an abundance of flowers will attract them in any quantity. Butterflies have distinct preferences among flowers, which must be types with accessible nectar. Valerian is an excellent butterfly flower and has a long season, from May to October or November. Buddleia is well known as the 'butterfly bush'; the best variety is the originally wild mauve one – the specially bred deep colours are less favoured, but white is usually well covered with butterflies. After Buddleia in attractiveness comes *Sedum spectabile*, the Ice Plant. Garden Vanessids, in particular Small Tortoiseshells, are very fond of it, and I have counted forty butterflies on a single plant. The right variety has pale pink flowers and is seldom more than a foot tall. The one most often offered by nurserymen is 'Autumn Joy', which is a deeper pink and grows to at least twice the height; its flowers are differently constructed, having no petals, and butterflies seldom visit it.

Late summer brings another important butterfly flower, the Michaelmas Daisy. At this time of year, garden butterflies are at their peak in numbers and are most in need of food to build up their strength for hibernation. However, it is also possible to encourage butterflies earlier in the year and to bring in species that would otherwise visit the garden infrequently. In spring, Sweet Rocket *(Hesperis matronalis)* provides nectar for the early species, and Orange Tips will lay on it, offering the gardener the chance to have a breeding colony of butterflies. *Hesperis* is a short-lived perennial which, like the Wallflower (another suitable nectar flower), is best grown as a biennial and replaced after the first year of flowering. Alyssum and Aubretia are visited by the earliest butterflies as, to a lesser extent, is the Primrose. Suitable plants to attract butterflies in early and mid summer include Catmint, Phlox, Sweet William, Lavender and Heliotrope.

Large gardens will also accommodate wild plants that butterflies need. Brimstones will search out Buckthorn bushes and lay on them if they are in a quiet corner. Let some Dandelions flourish in areas of long grass; they are probably the most useful nectar flowers from March to May. Some gardens provide ideal breeding sites for the nettle-eating Vanessids. If one or two patches are reserved for Stinging Nettles, part, at least, needs to be cut in late May or early June if it has no caterpillars on it; otherwise later broods will not lay on the tough, old shoots. Small Coppers and Common Blues will breed on long grass in gardens, and Speckled Woods do well in wild, preferably slightly damp corners that are partly shaded by trees or shrubs. Where the size and layout of the garden allow, wild flowers, which might otherwise be evicted as weeds, can be grown for the benefit of butterflies. Among the most useful of the wild flowers are Hemp Agrimony, Moon Daisy, Thistles and other Compositae, as well as Bramble, Clover and Campion. On chalky ground, Marjoram, Scabious and Knapweed are particularly useful.

It is more difficult for owners of country estates or large pieces of land to increase the butterfly population over a wide area. Merely releasing new stocks is likely to be a waste of effort and money. First, the butterflies and plants that already exist on the land need to be recorded in detail, so that the strengths of the populations may be assessed. This is one of the objectives of the British Butterfly Conservation Society's Habitat Surveys. The most rewarding policy will probably be the encouragement of species that are already successful rather than the introduction of new ones. In any case, new introductions should belong only to widespread species, not to local geographical races. Migrants like the Red Admiral and Clouded Yellow are not worth introducing as they do not establish permanent colonies. Any stage of the life cycle can be released, but the best results are usually achieved by freeing the adults or putting down larvae on suitable foodplants.

Above all, do not introduce foreign races of species on the British list. The temptation to release continental White Admirals, Purple Emperors and Swallowtails must be resisted as these are distinct geographical forms which would damage British wild populations if they were allowed to mix. Anyone who has plans to augment wild butterfly populations with introduced insects should first contact conservation bodies or the County Naturalists' Trusts (whose address can be obtained from the local public library). Such organisations should be able to make sure that any introduction scheme does not interfere with other scientific work and to provide advice on any natural conditions that might work against the scheme.

Until quite recently, butterflies were mainly viewed as items to collect – an attitude to be seen in almost every butterfly book that has been published. There is still much to be learned about the ecological requirements of butterflies and about the details of their lives at every stage of their development. Butterfly watching can teach us a lot about them, particularly as many species can be bred in captivity. Much valuable study has been carried out in the past by naturalists and indeed by collectors, but with butterfly populations diminishing each year, even inexperienced helpers can quickly become useful to the conservation societies in their work of preventing undesirable development, carrying out practical conservation schemes and generally educating the public. Without putting effort into conservation, we may have little pleasure from butterflies in the future.

This book is an appreciation of butterflies by an exceptional artist whose skill in depicting the wildlife that he observes is unsurpassed. Gordon Beningfield's paintings show his ability as a field naturalist and his feeling for the butterflies and plants that he portrays. Each butterfly is evoked in its natural surroundings with such precision that it should inspire anyone with the enthusiasm to go out and look for it in the wild.

Robert Goodden
Over Compton
Sherborne
Dorset
January 1978

ARTIST'S INTRODUCTION

I like to work directly from life whether I'm painting butterflies or other wildlife. In the field, I do a lot of drawings and watercolour notes to capture an immediate impression of the subject. I'm not too worried about detail, or about accuracy of size or texture when I'm sketching.

The painting is built up from these sketches, but made to go very much the way I want. Just because I have a natural subject, I do not feel forced to illustrate it exactly as it was – I try to paint it the way I saw it.

I like to use textured, hand-made paper, although it is now becoming difficult to find. The paper is always tinted, because I do not want to waste time fighting against white. The painting is started with as much freedom as I can give it. I saturate the paper with water and apply the washes and tones while it is very wet. As it dries, I apply any other colour or texture which I feel is necessary, bearing in mind the butterfly and the habitat around it.

When I'm happy with the colour and texture, I let the paper dry completely. I then set about painting the subject, superimposing it on the background that I have created. I treat it freely, using a large brush and painting as quickly as possible. Again, I let the picture dry before picking out whatever excites me from those quick shapes, perhaps of leaves or grasses, but letting some stay very muted, until finally my eye is concentrated on the main subject, the butterfly. The painting starts right at the back and comes forward to the sharp, life-size butterfly. The only body colour in these pictures is white used as a base over which I glaze the watercolours. Painting the butterfly first in white body colour gives it a glow and lifts it up from all the colours beneath. I also use the white for highlights in general, for flowers and fruit, to bring out the highlights in grasses, the iridescence of petals or the shine of leaves.

By holding the pencil or brush loosely in my hand, I don't restrict it, and the lines become very delicate. When the painting or drawing is almost doing itself, I know it is coming out right. I feel a little like a child with a painting book which just needs a paint brush and clear water to make the pictures come up in brilliant colour. Once I get that sort of feeling, I know I'm on the right lines. I like to make the backgrounds emphasise the area behind a leaf or a branch or a butterfly, leaving the main subject almost to come by itself.

If I have to struggle with a picture, it becomes laboured. The best thing to do then is tear it up and start again. After I have struggled with something, I can often solve the problems in seconds by starting afresh.

I use cabinet specimens of butterflies for colour and size. My measurements, which are made with a small pair of dividers, are not just of the size of the wing, but of the areas of colour – where one patch of scales ends and another starts. These measurements allow me to show the plumage of the wing accurately. For details which cabinet specimens do not provide – position, texture and the colour of the eyes – I work from life.

Butterflies, more than any other animals or plants, sum up for me the spirit of the English countryside in summer. But the England of quiet lanes and undisturbed hedgerows is disappearing fast. My paintings try to communicate my feelings about the unspoilt countryside while it is still there to be seen. Perhaps, if my pictures are successful in evoking the beauty and delicacy of butterflies, they will help a little towards encouraging their conservation.

Gordon Beningfield
Water End
Hertfordshire
April 1978

THE PLATES

BRIMSTONE

Gonepteryx rhamni Linnaeus 1758

Only the male has the bright yellow colour from which came its old name, Sulphur, and its current name, Brimstone. The female is greenish white on the upper side and in flight is hard to distinguish from the Whites. The pale undersides of both sexes are sufficiently leaflike to afford them some protection when they are sheltering in hibernation among evergreen foliage, particularly that of Ivy.

Emerging in the earliest sunny days of February, the Brimstone is the first of our butterflies to be seen at the end of the winter. It is common and almost evenly distributed across England and Wales, but becomes less abundant in the northern counties, in Scotland and in Ireland. Its distribution is largely determined by that of its two foodplants, Purging Buckthorn *(Rhamnus catharticus)* and Alder Buckthorn *(Frangula alnus)*. Brimstones fly some distance from their breeding territory; in my garden, they now breed wild every year on specially planted bushes, although I know of only one small wild Buckthorn bush within a radius of several miles.

The eggs are laid singly on terminal shoots, and the same shoot may sometimes be selected by several females. The slender green caterpillar at first conceals itself along the veins of a leaf. Later, it develops a smooth, matt texture with pale shading along the sides which helps it melt into its background of leaves – a vital characteristic as the caterpillar takes up an odd, humped posture, often on a very exposed leaf. The leaf-green chrysalis has prominent wing cases very like Buckthorn leaves. Nevertheless, except in captivity, it is not found attached to the foodplant. The caterpillar wanders off and pupates in other dense vegetation some distance away.

The Brimstone occurs in its greatest numbers, not in spring, but during July and August. Then, in a good year, the chrysalides that have developed from spring-laid eggs give rise to clouds of butterflies, which seem to prefer feeding from mauve or purplish flowers. After a summer peak, the numbers dwindle until only the few which have survived the ordeal of hibernation are left to breed in the spring.

Brimstone
amidst Ivy.

GK.

Brimstone
This was the first butterfly I painted after I decided to paint for a book. It was early in the year – late March, perhaps. I just strolled around the garden, where there is a mass of ivy, and the Brimstones were starting to move around on it. I did not say to myself that as there was a lot of green in the background the picture had to be like that. I didn't want to produce an illustration but to convey my ideas through the subject and conjure up the atmosphere and the time of year that I saw the butterfly in. G.B.

ORANGE TIP
Anthocharis cardamines Linnaeus 1758

Orange Tips are shown here on one of their favourite flowers, the Lady's Smock or Cuckoo Flower *(Cardamine pratensis)*, from which the species takes its scientific name. They frequent the damp water meadows where the Lady's Smock is in flower by early May, appearing just as spring is beginning to warm up. The Orange Tip is even more typical of country lanes and hedgerows, where the other main foodplant, Garlic Mustard *(Alliaria petiolata)*, grows. When the butterfly rests with wings closed on the inflorescences of small white flowers, it is effectively camouflaged by the mottled green and white pattern of its underside. The larvae, too, are remarkably adapted to living on the Garlic Mustard. They are slender and smooth, green in colour and with white counter-shading along the sides that makes them seem even slimmer and more like the very elongated seed pods which they prefer to the leaves as their food.

Eggs are laid singly near the calyx of the flower and turn from white to bright orange within hours. The cannibalistic inclinations of the caterpillars are far from unique – they have the function in nature of reducing the chance that all the caterpillars might perish because the food supply has been exhausted. Orange Tips can be encouraged to breed naturally in the wilder parts of a garden where they will lay prolifically on the buds and flowers of Sweet Rocket *(Hesperis matronalis)*.

There is a single brood each year on the wing from May, often into July. The next generation reaches the chrysalis stage in time for hibernation. The slender, spiky shape of the chrysalides makes them inconspicuous in the hedgerows. Although most of them are fawn, quite a number are green, and no satisfactory explanation has been advanced for the colour difference.

Only the male butterfly has the orange tips to the forewings. In all other respects, however, the female is similar. The green mottling on the underside of both sexes is not quite as it appears: a good lens will reveal that there is not a scrap of green on them and that the colour is produced by a mixture of black and yellow scales.

Background to have a pinkish orange tone

Orange - tip on Cuckoo flower

Orange Tip

The Orange Tip is one of my favourite butterflies. It reminds me of early summer and the English countryside, but my personal taste wouldn't allow me to have orange against the brilliant green of spring vegetation. During a lunch break when I was thinking about painting this picture of the Orange Tip on Cuckoo Flower, I was eating peach yoghurt, and it seemed a delightful colour. The colour range of orange with pink and buff and cream through to gentle browns all started with the peach yoghurt.   G.B.

BROWN ARGUS
Aricia agestis Schiffermueller 1775

In spite of its name, the Brown Argus is really one of the Blues; it lives among them and is very similar to them in its underside pattern of rings and spots. The sexes are alike, with chocolate brown uppersides, but the orange marginal spots are more prominent on the upperside of the female, and the male has more angular wings.

The Brown Argus, shown here with the rarer Small Blue, is found on downlands and other grassy habitats where the caterpillars live on Rockrose *(Helianthemum chamaecistus)* or Storksbill *(Erodium cicutarium)*. There are two flight periods each summer, with the first brood emerging in May and June while the second continues from July to September. In the North and in cooler years, there may be a single brood from June until August. The Brown Argus spends the winter as a half-grown caterpillar.

SMALL BLUE
Cupido minimus Fuessly 1775

The Small Blue confines itself to very small areas, although they may contain only small amounts of its foodplant; even the flight of the butterflies may be restricted to within a few metres of their breeding place. Such a limitation of range is unique among British butterflies.

Although the Small Blue is not a rarity, it is decidedly localised in its occurrence, commoner in the south and hardly seen north of the Midlands. It is a butterfly of chalk and limestone hillsides where its foodplant is the Kidney Vetch or Ladies' Fingers *(Anthyllis vulneraria)*.

The larva bores into a flowerhead, feeding throughout the late summer until it is fully developed and ready to pupate. First, however, it hibernates among the dead flowerheads and it does not change into the chrysalis until April or May. The first butterflies emerge in May, and the flight is usually over by the end of June. In hot summers, some of the caterpillars pupate and produce a partial second brood of adults in late August or September.

Our smallest butterfly, it is easily told from other downland Blues by the absence of orange spots from the underside, which is grey with black flecks. The uppersides of the wings are charcoal; only in the male is the colour lightened with a dusting of slate blue.

Brown Argus
+ Small Blue

Bank of
speedwell

GB

Brown Argus and Small Blue
I wanted to show these two little butterflies deep down in their environment. First of all, I was attracted by a bank of blue Speedwell flowers. I was in an area near my home where there are Small Blues. A lot of them were flying around. As I was hoping to see either a Small Blue or an Argus on the Speedwell, I stood around there for half an hour or so. Then both species landed on it. That clinched it for me. I did a quick drawing and painted the picture almost as I saw it, although I have influenced the surrounding colours, as I always do, to suit my taste.   G.B.

MARBLED WHITE
Melanargia galathea Linnaeus 1758

As its name suggests, the Marbled White resembles the members of the Pieridae in its white colour and black markings. It is, however, a member of the Satyridae, the only one in Britain without the usual brown or ochre colour; it does have the swollen veins at the base of the forewing and the eye-like markings that are characteristic of the Satyridae.

The Marbled White is a butterfly of chalk and limestone grasslands in southern England, with very few colonies further north. It forms widely scattered colonies, sometimes occupying a stretch of bank only a few metres long and miles away from any other group.

The eggs are scattered by the female at random among the grass and hatch to produce almost microscopic larvae which immediately go into hibernation on dead grass. In spring, they feed mainly on Sheep's Fescue Grass *(Festuca ovina)*. The adults emerge in July.

SMALL SKIPPER
Thymelicus sylvestris Poda 1761

A freshly emerged Small Skipper butterfly has the unblemished velvety texture which is depicted here. Found at the edges of woodland, on grassy verges and downland, the Small Skipper takes as its foodplants such soft grasses as Timothy and Catstail. The caterpillar hibernates before starting to feed, building itself a white silken hibernaculum for the winter. The chrysalis is formed inside a loosely spun cocoon of grass and silk, which is unusual in butterflies, though typical of Skippers, a curious and primitive family which taxonomists in the past have treated as a sub-order separate from butterflies and moths, and of equal status in classification.

The butterfly emerges in late June and will be seen until early September. It is very similar to the rarer Essex Skipper, which was not recognised as a separate species until 1890. The main difference lies in the antennae, which are black-tipped on the underside in the Essex but entirely orange underneath in the Small Skipper. Males of both species have a prominent line of scent scales on the forewing, while the females are unmarked.

marbled white

Harebells

GB.

Marbled White and Small Skipper
The starting point for this picture was a windy day on the Chilterns near Ivinghoe. There were Harebells blowing in the wind, and I was lucky enough to see the Marbled Whites and the Skippers on them. With the cool colours of the Marbled White and the Harebells, it was natural for the background to take on a cool tone. The only warmth which naturally came in was the Small Skipper.   G.B.

SMALL COPPER
Lycaena phlaeas Linnaeus 1761

The Small Copper is unusual among the members of the family Lycaenidae in being rather solitary by nature. The highly territorial male is so pugnacious that it will chase away others, not just of its own kind, but also Blues and Small Heaths. As an adult, it is very active, flying swiftly in short hops. It will often alight on a bare patch of soil or on a green stem rather than on the flowers that most butterflies prefer.

In the open, grassy places that it likes, the Small Copper is widespread throughout Britain, though most common in the south. Its iridescent copper colouring is shared by only one other British butterfly, the Large Copper, which is confined to reserves. The wing markings are extremely variable, and a common form, *caeruleopunctata,* has iridescent blue spots along the inner margin of the hindwing. Sexual differences are obscured by the extent of the natural variation, but the female has less angular forewings than the male and has a slight tail to the hindwing.

The eggs are laid on Sheep's Sorrel *(Rumex acetosella)*, sometimes several to a leaf. The caterpillar eats a hole its own size in the cuticle and settles down in the depression. As it is flat and pale green, it is difficult to find until it eats, leaving behind it a trail where the leaf is stripped to a transparent membrane. When it is larger, the caterpillar eats the leaf right through and rests closely pressed against the midrib. At this stage, it is edged with a maroon colour which matches the markings on the leaves. Dock, on which the caterpillar will also feed, has similar markings.

With three and sometimes four overlapping broods in a year, the Small Copper may be seen from April to November. Before they hibernate, the young caterpillars turn the colour of withered leaves; in spring, they become green again.

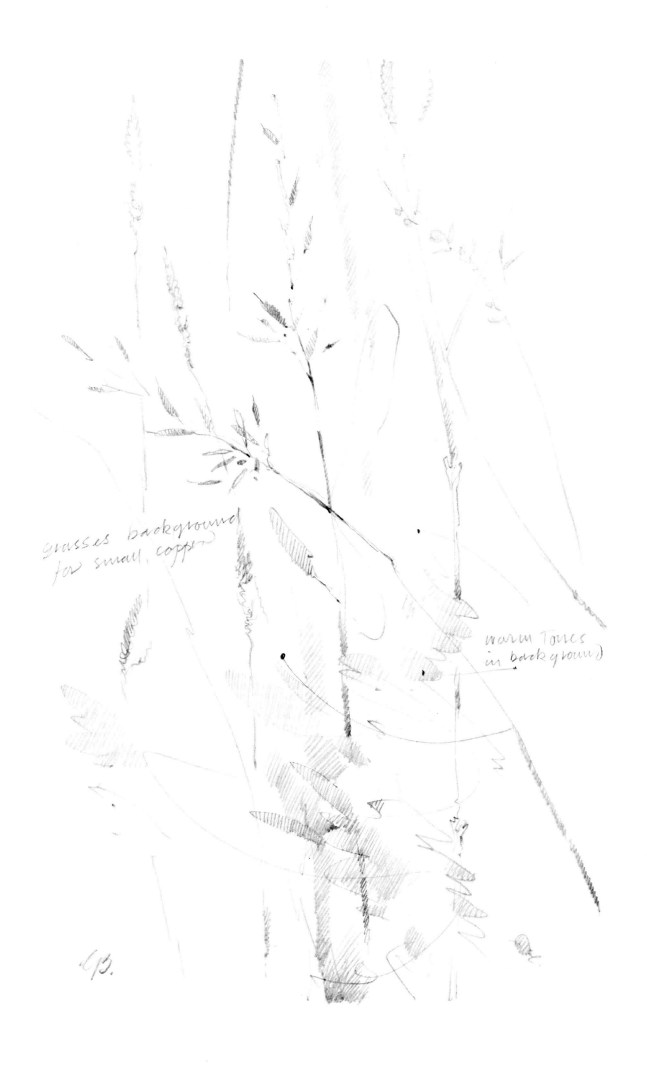

grasses background
for small copper

warm tones
in background

LB.

small Copper
in grasses

Background
warm in colour

Small Copper
The background here is warm to be in harmony with the main
subject of the butterfly. If a painting like this is rather hot, I like
to develop the depth in it as a way of bringing in a little coolness.
I've enjoyed myself with the Bindweed which works its way
round grasses and other plants to create an exciting, sculptural
effect. The Small Copper and the Bindweed are both found in
front of my house. G.B.

GREEN HAIRSTREAK
Callophrys rubi Linnaeus 1758

When this vivacious little butterfly settles on the foliage among which it is normally found, it becomes almost invisible. The green colour, unique among British butterflies, is restricted to the underside, and the brown of the upperside is exposed only on the infrequent occasions when the butterfly spreads its wings to bask in the sun. The male differs externally from the female only in having small, oval patches of pale scent scales on the leading edges of the forewings.

The Green Hairstreak and related species spend a lot of their time walking and wheeling about on foliage. On landing, they adopt a head-downwards position with the hindwings held prominently out and rotating in a curious fashion which makes the tails move as if they were waving antennae. This habit may help at least those species of Hairstreak whose wings have longer tails to escape from predatory birds, which are likely to take a stab at the wrong end of the butterfly and finish up with only a beakful of wing.

This is the commonest of our Hairstreaks and is most likely to be found on dry, grassy scrub and heathland. As the females lay their eggs on a number of shrubby plants, hedgerows and the wooded edges of meadows will often provide a suitable habitat for the Green Hairstreak. Gorse is probably the most favoured among a surprisingly wide range of foodplants including Dogwood, Heather, both species of Buckthorn, Birdsfoot Trefoil, Rockrose and many clovers, vetches and trefoils.

The eggs are laid singly, close to a flowering shoot. If two caterpillars hatch out on the same shoot, one is likely to eat the other, removing the competition for the food supply. The young caterpillar bores into the centre of the flower and feeds from any part of it, including the petals. It has the ability to take on the colour of its surroundings and can remain quite inconspicuous even when it has shed its skin three times and is so large that it can no longer remain inside a flower or fruit.

The Green Hairstreak is unusual among British butterflies in hibernating as a chrysalis. The adults begin to emerge in April or, usually, May and the single brood remains on the wing until well into July.

Green Hairstreak.
The butterfly is engulfed
in a secret green world.

Green Hairstreak

We are very lucky to have Green Hairstreaks locally, and I see them often in Dorset. When its wings are closed, it is a green butterfly in a lovely green world of leaves – an irresistible subject for me. The contrasting colours, such as the greyish blue at the bottom of this painting, are introduced towards the end when I feel the need to bring in my own colour balance and to adjust the composition.   G.B.

WHITE ADMIRAL
Ladoga camilla Linnaeus 1763

This is one of our finest butterflies, as its old name of White Admirable suggested. Its usual haunts are mature deciduous woodlands, generally those which include oak trees. The White Admiral often accompanies the rarer Purple Emperor, but it is one of the few species that are actually increasing, with the localities where it is found becoming more widespread across southern England and the Midlands.

The flight of these majestic butterflies leaves an unforgettable impression as they swoop down from a height and up again with a few fast wingbeats. They are usually found in groups, particularly in woodland clearings or along the edges of rides. The flowers to which they are most attracted are those of the Bramble; in some places, one may come upon as many as a score of White Admirals around a Bramble bush.

After early emergences near the end of June, the White Admiral is on the wing for most of July and into August. The females leave the main group and go into the undergrowth to lay their eggs singly on honeysuckle leaves. The caterpillar, which has an odd habit of covering itself in dry particles of its own excreta, takes up a position at the tip of a leaf as if it were an extension of the midrib. It feeds at night, returning to the tip each morning.

For the winter, the caterpillar, which is still quite small, makes an intricate hibernaculum by spinning silk round the plant stem and the leaf stalk, so that the leaf cannot fall in autumn. It then wraps the remaining part of the leaf around itself as a withered, perfectly camouflaged refuge for the winter. Early the following summer, before pupation, it has become a handsome bright green with prominent maroon spikes. The chrysalis, too, is spectacular: it is green with reflective silver patches and with forked protuberances at the head, which is downwards as the chrysalis hangs by the tail deep among the foliage.

The male butterflies are discernibly blacker and have slightly less rounded wings than the otherwise similar females. Rare examples occur with the white band reduced to a pale marking (variety *semi-nigrina*), and the even rarer variety *nigrina* has black wings without a trace of white.

White Admiral on bramble.

Pink bramble blossom

cobweb

White Admiral

White Admirals are not found near my home in Hertfordshire but I have seen them around the New Forest. They often fly over brambles, and the combination makes a good subject. I like the texture of the thorns and the pink colour of the flowers – I was able to bring together pink and brown, two colours of which I am very fond. The cobwebs were woven round dead fruit from the previous year.   G.B.

COMMON BLUE
Polyommatus icarus Rottemburg 1775

In unusually hot years, Common Blues will be found in gardens and waysides as well as in their usual habitat of downlands and grassy meadows. While dense colonies are now seldom seen, this butterfly remains the most prolific of our Blues and may still appear in hundreds, even thousands, in a particular locality.

As you walk through grassland in summer, the adults take flight and move busily from place to place, hovering as if to alight and then passing on to a more suitable flower or grass stem. In the evenings, they congregate in sheltered pockets, often at the bottom of a slope, where they rest, heads downwards and wings closed, in a characteristic position, sometimes several of them to a single grass stem. Although this can make them rather conspicuous, in the fading light their forms do resemble the flowering heads of grasses, notably of Cocksfoot.

Among the many clovers, trefoils and vetches on which they lay their eggs, the most favoured foodplant is Birdsfoot Trefoil *(Lotus corniculatus)*. The caterpillar of the Common Blue is green and tapers at each end rather like a woodlouse – the typical shape of caterpillars in the family Lycaenidae. Sweet secretion from a honey gland at the posterior attracts ants which attend the larva almost incessantly. There are normally two broods in a season; in warm years, a third brood emerges as butterflies in September or even October. As the broods overlap, Common Blues are to be seen continuously from May to September.

The species can be distinguished from the rather similar Adonis Blue by its slightly violet shade and by the pure white borders to the wings; in the Adonis, the black venation of the wings cuts into the borders. As in most Blues, only the male has the attractive blue colour, and the female is dark brown on the upperside. Irish and some Scottish forms have large, extra brightly coloured males. Their females have a great deal of blue, and the wings are edged with vivid orange lunules.

common blue
on Goat's beard

Common Blue
I suppose it is because I have produced quite a lot of sculpture that I find any seeds of wild flowers particularly fascinating. I love their apparent lack of colour, although actually there is plenty of very subtle colour in them. Blues are probably my favourite butterflies, but for me the Goatsbeard alone would make a painting in its own right. There was plenty of it around in my jungle garden. Again, all I had to do was draw the seeds and wait for the Common Blue to come. In most of my paintings, I think of the butterfly, which I want to portray as accurately as possible, and then let myself go with the background with stylised colours and textures that I hope represent the world of the butterfly in a free, painterly way.   G.B.

ADONIS BLUE

Lysandra bellargus Rottemburg 1775

The Adonis Blue is rapidly becoming scarcer: it is now exceedingly local and found no further north than the mouth of the River Severn. Its habitats are calcareous hills and downlands on which its sole foodplant, the Horseshoe Vetch *(Hippocrepis comosa)*, grows. The colonies of the Adonis Blue are not as dense as those of the Chalkhill Blue, and some of them are restricted to a small area of escarpment.

The two broods each year are separated by a clear gap: after the first, which appears in May and lasts into June, no more butterflies are seen until the second emergence early in August. The female lays on the leaves and stems of the foodplant. Larvae from eggs laid in the spring develop through five instars to pupate in July in a loose cocoon of silk which rests on the ground. The larvae of the second brood stop feeding at the third instar and hibernate attached to a pad of silk spun on the foodplant before going on to complete their development in the spring.

By far the brightest of all the Blues, the Adonis can also be recognised by the black veins which interrupt the prominent white fringe of the wings. The Common Blue, which is sometimes confused with the Adonis, is slightly lilac and less iridescent in comparison. The female Adonis is much darker than the female Chalkhill Blue: almost charcoal, with a suffusion of metallic blue scales which appears mainly around the body and is rather variable in extent. The major variation, though, is in the underside markings; this is less pronounced than in the Chalkhill Blue but was nevertheless a source of great interest among past generations of collectors. Rare female examples are blue all over like the males, if in a slightly different shade. These belong to form *ceronus*, which corresponds to a blue female form, known as *synagrapha,* in the Chalkhill.

Adonis Blue

GBeningfield

Adonis Blue

The Adonis Blue lives on lush, green, grassy downs. I have not found it in the Chilterns – this was in Dorset. I literally lay on my stomach to get down into the grassy world of the butterfly. The Adonis Blue is a remarkably attractive butterfly, with a unique, jewel-like blue colour in the male. I wanted to show as much of this as possible. However, I do not like opening the wings wide and flat, because it makes the butterflies look like cabinet specimens. So although I needed to show that this was an Adonis Blue as opposed to a Common Blue, I have still kept some perspective in the butterfly.   G.B.

CLOUDED YELLOW
Colias crocea Geoffroy 1785

The Clouded Yellow comes to Britain each summer in migrations across France from the Mediterranean region and North Africa. It is most often seen along the South Coast, but spreads northwards at least to the Midlands. The first arrivals, usually few in number, may appear as early as May or June. These insects breed here, and their progeny are joined in July and August by a further wave of migrants. The Clouded Yellow is therefore at its most plentiful in late summer and autumn. The great Clouded Yellow year was 1947, when hundreds of thousands arrived in a spectacular show of the species without equal here before or since.

The best places to look for Clouded Yellows are the fields of Clover and Lucerne which form their main breeding grounds. As well as laying their eggs on these two plants, the butterflies also take nectar from the flowers. In the South of France, Clover or Lucerne fields will attract hundreds of Clouded Yellows, but the numbers diminish further north; in Britain, they tend to be seen singly or in very small groups.

The bottle-shaped eggs, typical of the family Pieridae which also includes the Whites, are salmon pink shortly after being laid but change to black when ready to hatch. The smooth leaf-green caterpillar is well camouflaged on the midrib of a clover leaf. In warm weather, it is capable of rapid growth. The chrysalis is yellowish green, the colour of the stem to which it is attached. The Clouded Yellow is a continuously brooded butterfly with no winter stage in this country; adults may be encountered well into November in mild years. Cold weather, however, kills both the butterflies and their juvenile stages. The life cycle abroad slows down in the cooler months: the larvae may take two or three months instead of three or four weeks to mature, but there is no hibernation. Around the Mediterranean, Clouded Yellows can appear in February.

The feature which distinguishes the sexes is the presence in the female only of yellow spots in the dark margins of the wings. White replaces the yellow colouring completely in the form known as *helice*, which is restricted to females and forms a small proportion of every brood, although the percentage of *helice* females is higher in some strains than in others.

clover + white campion
possible situation
for - clouded Yellow

LB.

Clouded Yellow

Clover & white Campion

Clouded Yellow
I have not seen the Clouded Yellow in Hertfordshire recently.
Even in Dorset I have not seen it for a couple of years. As it is an
extremely vivid butterfly and frequents clover fields, I made this
a very colourful painting, using a group of meadow flowers –
Clover and White Campion. The spattering of cold colours is to
balance the warmth of the butterfly and the flowers.   G.B.

CHALKHILL BLUE
Lysandra coridon Poda 1761

The silvery paleness of this butterfly marks it out from the other British Blues. It is a grassland species which occurs only in South and Central England and is restricted to the calcareous pastures and cliffs where its main foodplant, Horseshoe Vetch *(Hippocrepis comosa)*, is found. However, the Chalkhill Blue has been found breeding on other leguminous plants such as Kidney Vetch *(Anthyllis vulneraria)* and Birdsfoot *(Ornithopus perpusillus)*.

The eggs are laid in July and August, not so much on the foodplant as on other plants nearby. The female walks among the stems, depositing eggs on them as she goes. The larva develops inside the eggshell but does not hatch until the spring. The young caterpillar is mainly green; later, it develops bright yellow patches which help it to merge into a background of yellow *Hippocrepis* flowers.

Apart from marked sexual dimorphism (the female is soft grey-brown instead of blue), there is also great variation in the colouring and marking of both sexes, particularly on the underside. The variations in the spots, rings and orange chevrons have been the subject of detailed study by collectors who, in the past, have amassed cabinets full of the aberrations of the Chalkhill Blue.

Within its range, the butterfly is still common and found in dense colonies, but the number of colonies has decreased and the Chalkhill Blue is seldom seen in the profusion that was taken for granted earlier this century.

The butterflies feed from almost every flower in their vicinity, but spend a great deal of their time basking with wings open on stones, rocks or bare soil. The single brood is on the wing from the second week of July until some time in September.

chalkhill blue

C.B.

chalkhill Blue

Chalkhill Blue

Chalkhill Blues have the same habitat as Adonis Blues, but we
have them in abundance where I live. When I'm sketching in the
field, I refuse to let myself be held up by any preconceptions
about the way the painting is going to be. Sometimes I use it
almost unaltered; on other occasions, I take an area of the original
drawing that I particularly enjoy and balance the painting up to
suit myself. This picture is very close to my sketch. The grasses
appeal to me because they are in miniature like armatures for
sculpture.   G.B.

DARK GREEN FRITILLARY
Mesoacidalia aglaja Linnaeus 1758

This large Fritillary is capable of great speed, but usually flies quite low and often settles where it can be watched closely. Away from patches of thistles, whose flowers may attract a dozen or so in quite a small area, the Dark Green Fritillary is usually seen singly. It likes open but scrubby grassland, particularly chalk or limestone downs, and is found in scattered localities from the south up to Scotland and the Hebrides. In this rather variable butterfly, the females are darker than the males, and there are particularly dark forms in the north and at high altitudes. It can easily be confused with the rarer High Brown Fritillary but has a distinct green background to the silver spots on the underside, where the High Brown has clearer, brighter spangles on maroon or chestnut.

The eggs are laid in July on Violet and hatch in two or three weeks into larvae which go straight into hibernation among the foliage without feeding at all. The fully grown caterpillars are black and very prickly, with red spots along the sides. The chrysalis hangs in a puparium formed from vegetation and produces the butterfly after about a month, in early July.

SMALL HEATH
Coenonympha pamphilus Linnaeus 1758

This little butterfly may be abundant in meadows and almost any kind of grassland. It appears in May. In the north, there is only one brood, lasting into July or August, but over most of the country a second brood keeps a succession of Small Heaths on the wing until October.

Of the first brood larvae, some develop fast and produce adults in August or September. These adults lay eggs which hatch into larvae that hibernate when quite small. The rest of the first brood larvae develop more slowly and are well grown before hibernation; they pupate in the early spring and become the first adults to appear at the start of the season.

Dark Green Fritillary
Small Heath

SB.

Dark Green Fritillary and Small Heath

I was in a rough, meadowy area on the edge of a wood. There were Small Heaths everywhere on the mass of Ragwort, which I was sketching, when the Dark Green Fritillary settled on it. This coincidental combination of colours gave me the idea for the painting. I emphasised the yellowness by dropping the leaves out almost completely, because the world of the butterfly is very close. Observing it as I sketched put me in its minute world: all I could see was the sunburst of yellow, and that is how the painting came out.   G.B.

PAINTED LADY
Vanessa cardui Linnaeus 1758

An accomplished migrant, the Painted Lady has succeeded in establishing itself on every continent of the world. As the butterflies do not survive the British winter, the presence of Painted Ladies in this country depends on the arrival each spring of immigrants from the countries around the Mediterranean.

The main foodplant is Thistle, although the larvae will also eat other plants including Stinging Nettle and Burdock. The eggs are laid singly on leaves, and the young larva lives solitarily on the under surface, making a shelter by drawing the leaf edges together with silken strands. At first, the caterpillar eats the leaf surface without biting right through, but later it is completely exposed. The caterpillar, which is black with yellow markings and prickly spines, constructs another shelter of leaves bound with silk in which to pupate. Inside, it hangs by the tail and changes to a chrysalis which develops quickly, producing the butterfly in seven to ten days.

The Painted Lady flies fast and purposefully in a way that is instantly recognisable to the lepidopterist, even at a distance. It is wary, quickly taking flight if approached, although the butterfly may be observed more closely if it is engrossed in taking nectar from flowers. It often behaves territorially, returning if disturbed to more or less the same spot after circling round at great speed. Unlike the Red Admiral, it prefers flowers to the juices of rotting fruit; it is a butterfly of fields and gardens rather than of orchards. Painted Ladies are usually seen, at most, in very small numbers. In some years, they are not uncommon, but it is possible for a summer to go by with hardly any sightings. Elsewhere in the world, the Painted Lady can live in large colonies, but the numbers thin out before they reach our shores.

It is the progeny of the May arrivals that are most commonly met with; they are at their peak in July and August. As the Painted Lady does not hibernate, the butterflies breed continuously into the autumn, when the early stages are killed by the low temperatures, strong winds and dampness.

Painted lady

clover

Ox eye - daisy

YB

*Painted lady
on clover & Ox-eye Daisy*

Painted Lady

On the day that I saw the Painted Lady settle on Ox-eye Daisies, the weather was dull. That and the depth of vegetation on the bank where the daisies were growing meant that the flowers were rather shrouded and enclosed. Had it been sunny, they would have been a brilliant white, and I would probably not have been attracted to them as a subject. The jungle feeling, which is an important part of the butterfly world, is strong here with the bold flowers, and there is so much to compete with the butterfly that I would have needed to use as striking a butterfly as a Painted Lady even if I hadn't seen it there.   G.B.

PEACOCK
Inachis io Linnaeus 1758

The Peacock emerges from its chrysalis in July, and it is at this time that the species is most numerous – it is common in the south of England but rarer in the north and absent from most of Scotland. The butterflies feed avidly before they hibernate and are attracted into gardens, above all by the flowers of Buddleia. In their natural haunts of woodland clearings and open country, they visit many types of flower but show a preference for Lucerne, Thistle, Knapweed, Clover and Marjoram. In the second half of July, some woodlands are positively crowded with Peacocks and Brimstones, jostling with Fritillaries and Whites to take advantage of the abundance of nectar that is available.

Peacocks begin to hibernate in August, but some are still flying in October. When a Peacock opens its wings, there is an audible rustle or scraping sound; if a group of hibernating Peacocks is disturbed, the noise may be enough to deter a predator. The first butterflies emerge from hibernation in March and April, when they are often attracted to feed from Pussy Willow catkins.

The only foodplant of the Peacock is the Stinging Nettle. The eggs are laid near the growing tip of a young nettle, pyramidally stacked in a dense, green mass. The larvae, which hatch simultaneously, live together inside a web of silk which is spun over the head of the nettle. Eventually, like Small Tortoiseshell caterpillars, they sit in a dense mass on the outside of the web, looking very conspicuous. As they grow, they move their quarters, spinning new webs as they go. They are jet black, prominently spined and covered with pinpoints of white. Their chestnut brown claspers or false legs distinguish them from Small Tortoiseshell caterpillars.

The groups stay close together until they are about to pupate. They then split up quite suddenly. Within a few hours, all except the odd straggler have left the nettle bed. They will travel quite a distance to find a suitably secluded spot for pupation. The chrysalides are a grained and mottled grey-brown colour, but those reared in captivity are pale green flecked with purple or maroon.

Peacock.
a dark tone overall
the background

cobweb

gb.

Peacock

I saw a mass of mauve heads, but one of them was an eye looking at me. As an abstract shape, the round eye on the butterfly had to relate to all the thistle heads, but with the bright eye looking out from a very cool background. I could not have opened the Peacock up any further, partly as a matter of taste and partly because it would have detracted from my conception of the picture.   G.B.

SMALL TORTOISESHELL
Aglais urticae Linnaeus 1758

The Small Tortoiseshell is less common in most parts of Europe than it is in the British Isles, where it is one of the most plentiful and widespread butterflies. Almost anywhere that its sole foodplant, the Stinging Nettle, grows, the Small Tortoiseshell will breed. It can be encouraged to breed naturally in large gardens by finding places where nettles can be allowed to grow in full sunlight. The females will normally lay only on tender shoots; the nettles must be scythed or grazed in early June to provide suitable vegetation for the butterflies that lay in the late summer.

The green eggs are laid in a tight cluster under a leaf near the terminal shoot of the nettle. From the hundreds of eggs laid on a single plant develop larvae which live gregariously almost until pupation. They stay tightly packed inside a fine web of silk which engulfs several leaves, moving only when they have eaten the food supply within. Leaving a trail of silk behind them, they then go off to spin a larger shelter on another shoot. When they are too big to be enclosed in this way, they sit quite prominently in a black mass. When disturbed, they raise their heads in perfect unison and emit beads of a greeny, sticky substance that is bitter to taste. Although this helps protect them against birds and other predators, many do get eaten and still more are parasitised by ichneumon flies.

The larvae scatter before pupating and choose as their shelters hedges, hollow trees, holes in rock faces or crevices in buildings. Like the Peacock, the Small Tortoiseshell in captivity pupates on the foodplant and forms a chrysalis of a different colour from that found in the wild – here largely metallic gold instead of dull, mottled brown.

There are two or even three broods in a year, with the first eggs being laid by butterflies that have hibernated from the previous autumn. The butterflies are most abundant in August and September, after successful summer breeding. Before hibernation, these butterflies require plentiful nectar to build up their endurance. It is at this time that they are so plentiful in gardens, where they feed especially on *Sedum spectabile*, Buddleia and Michaelmas Daisy. The survivors from hibernation are on the wing again in March.

Small Tortoiseshell
I'm used to seeing Small Tortoiseshells on most vegetation, but on this occasion, I came out of a very shady wood to a small clearing to see these two Small Tortoiseshells resting on the ground in a spot of sunlight, drinking up the warmth. I painted them almost as I saw them. The butterflies and the stones made a good composition and the rest of the picture followed from it, with just an indication of the edge of the woodland behind and a freely painted area of textured colour in the foreground.   G.B.

PURPLE HAIRSTREAK
Quercusia quercus Linnaeus 1758

When the Purple Hairsteak has its wings closed, it is silver-grey, the bright, iridescent royal blue or purple of the upperside is seen only when the butterflies spread their wings to sun themselves. The female is black, with bars of intense purplish blue on the fore-wings. The whole upperside of the male's wings is a pale, shot purple, but in many lights this metallic colour is seen just on one side or the other, changing with the angle of vision.

This is not a rare Hairstreak but is greatly prized by lepidopterists. Old oakwoods are the best places to search for it. On occasion, the butterflies come down to flowers and they are particularly attracted to the sticky honeydew from aphids which covers much of the foliage in midsummer. But the butterflies may more often be seen in groups up in the treetops dancing and weaving around the growing tips of oak branches. These are butterflies to watch through binoculars.

When they land on leaves, Purple Hairstreaks walk around very actively, usually with a wheeling motion, flaunting the tail in a peculiar way. Also typical of the Hairstreaks is the resting posture, head down and with the hindwings rubbing together to make the tails move like antennae. There is a bright spot at the base of the tail which could act as a target, like an eye, to distract a predator.

Eggs are laid on oak twigs in July and August. They do not hatch until spring, at about the time when the oak buds begin to open. Should the eggs hatch first, the young caterpillars simply bore into the unopened buds and consume the contents. By the time the leaves are appearing, the caterpillar is roughly the same size, shape and colour as the expanded bud scales. The chrysalis is formed either in a crevice of bark or among debris on the ground. The single brood of butterflies lasts from the middle of July until September.

Purple
Hairstreak,

Purple Hairstreak
The setting here is the natural one for these butterflies, which fly around oak trees. Given the vast subject of an oak wood, I needed to isolate a part of it: I have used the perspective of a small branch coming towards me to create a composition. I have brought in some light, as if from the edge of the wood, and done away with some of the green which didn't appeal to me in this context. Behind the branch there is a fantasy world which suggests the rest of the habitat.   G.B.

MEADOW BROWN
Maniola jurtina Linnaeus 1758

Certainly among the commonest of our butterflies, the Meadow Brown will inhabit almost any wild, grassy place from sea level up to considerable altitudes. It is very variable in its markings, with several named geographical races and conspicuous differences even between individuals from the same locality. The female is easily recognisable because of the patches of orange, mainly on the fore-wing; the only markings on the upperside of the male are the small eye-spots and occasionally a slight suffusion of orange.

The eggs are laid on grasses, and the larvae hide low down in the grass by day, crawling up the stems to feed at night. They never actually hibernate but will take a little food on the milder days in winter. Growth becomes more rapid in the spring. The caterpillar pupates in May and the butterfly emerges after three to four weeks. The season lasts well into August with later specimens resulting from slow-developing larvae. There is sometimes a second brood in hot years.

RINGLET
Aphantopus hyperantus Linnaeus 1758

The dark chocolate colour of the Ringlet distinguishes it from the more widespread Meadow Brown. The Ringlet, which is scarce in the Midlands and North, prefers more sheltered places than the open country inhabited by the Meadow Brown.

It shares with the Marbled White the curious habit of scattering its eggs at random among grass rather than, like all other British butterflies, attaching them to the foodplant. It may do so in flight or while walking among the vegetation. The newly hatched larvae soon find their chosen foodplant – a coarse grass – and start to feed. Its annual cycle is like that of the Meadow Brown, but the adults emerge about a fortnight later. The Ringlet will fly more readily than the Meadow Brown on dull days and even in light drizzle. The butterfly has a characteristic lilting flight and seems completely unhurried if approached. The adults are particularly fond of Bramble, Wild Thyme and almost any Composite flower such as Thistle or Hawkweed.

Ringlet & Meadow Brown.

Hawksbeard,
soft impressions
of seeds,

Yb.

Meadow Brown and Ringlet
The seeds of the Hawksbeard allowed me to go off into a world of high summer and dryness, reminiscent of impressionist paintings. I was peering at the butterflies through a whirl of down. My natural vision sharpened up the subject I was studying, but I was very conscious of the softness of the downy seeds which gave the setting its atmosphere. The colours have the gentle quality of a hazy summer day; I don't like very hot, bright sun.   G.B.

RED ADMIRAL
Vanessa atalanta Linnaeus 1758

Almost any kind of habitat is suitable for the Red Admiral, which is common throughout the British Isles. It is a strong migrant: as with the Painted Lady, the British-bred butterflies each summer are the offspring of Mediterranean immigrants. There are recorded instances of Red Admirals hibernating in Britain, but these are exceptional.

New arrivals in May lay their eggs singly on Stinging Nettle leaves. The larvae live solitarily in a bulbous tent constructed by drawing the edges of a leaf together. The larvae are often parasitised and produce a dull, buzzing fly instead of a bright Red Admiral. The pupae are usually formed in nearby hedgerows or other dense cover. The May butterflies' offspring usually emerge in July, and Red Admirals will then be seen right through the autumn and even into December. This late in the year, they are particularly fond of ivy flowers on walls and banks exposed to the sunshine.

Because of their passion for many kinds of cultivated flower, especially Buddleia and Michaelmas Daisy, Red Admirals are often found in gardens, but they are as likely to be seen in open fields, woodlands and forest edges – in fact, wherever there are plenty of nectar-producing flowers for the adults and Nettles for the larvae. In autumn, the butterflies turn their attentions to ripe fruit and will be seen probing blackberries and other soft fruit. The Red Admiral is markedly territorial: if disturbed, the butterfly takes off and circles around, usually returning to the same spot.

The egg of the Red Admiral is pale green and barrel-shaped, with prominent longitudinal keels running down from the apex. The spiny caterpillars have a line of yellow crescents along each side and are surprisingly variable in colour from black through shades of brown or grey to green or almost white.

Red admiral
Blackberry o Rosehip.

GB.

Red Admiral

Red Admirals are a typically autumnal sight, although you do see them earlier in the year. Blackberries and rose hips, which I love to paint, capture for me the feeling of the English countryside in autumn, and I have used autumnal colours in the background. I have prevented the leaf forms from coming up strongly so that they do not jar against the striking and complicated pattern of the butterfly. I wanted to keep the main interest in the centre of the picture where my own eye was focussed.   G.B.

SMALL WHITE
Pieris rapae Linnaeus 1758

Found throughout the British Isles in every type of locality, the Small White is a pest which can spread very rapidly. It has become abundant in New Zealand, where it was accidentally introduced around 1929, and in Australia, where it arrived ten years later. Cabbages are the most important crop to suffer; the females will lay dozens of eggs on a single plant. The range of foodplants includes turnips and practically any other member of the Cruciferae.

Eggs laid in May produce a second generation of butterflies in July. Pupae are formed on or near the foodplant, with those of the second generation hiding in more sheltered places for hibernation. Warm summers may result in a third brood, and Small White butterflies can be around from February to November. They are most at home in woodland clearings and along country lanes, where they cause little or no damage. They prefer to feed from cruciferous flowers, but will visit almost any flower that secretes nectar.

GREEN-VEINED WHITE
Pieris napi Linnaeus 1758

Although White butterflies have a bad name, and the Green-Veined White flies with Cabbage Whites in the garden, it is not a pest. Its true home is in woodlands, along lanes and in damp meadows where it can find the cruciferous foodplants on which it lays its eggs. The butterfly can easily be recognised at rest by the heavy venation on the underside of its wings.

The lime green or yellow chrysalides, which may be formed on vegetation or on fences or walls, are among the first to give rise to butterflies each spring. In the second brood of each season, only some of the chrysalides develop into butterflies in the same summer while others remain dormant and hibernate to produce adults the following spring, sometimes as early as March.

LB,

the whole thing very
pale with almost an
opal quality.

Small & green-veined Whites

Small White and Green-Veined White
Thistledown is one of my favourite subjects – I let thistles grow
everywhere around my house. The thistle in this painting is
bursting and being stirred by the wind; I have used it almost like a
shining light. White butterflies and others do settle on broken
thistledown. I cannot think of anything more attractive than white
butterflies on a white background, giving a very ethereal feeling
about them. I have used one or two of the last, lingering flowerheads to bring in a tiny bit of colour. This is a soft, gently moving
subject.   G.B.

COMMA
Polygonia c-album Linnaeus 1758

The Comma will often remain for long periods basking in strong sunshine with its wings spread and flattened against a leaf. In this position, the curious, serrated shape of the wings and the richness of its colour make it a striking sight. But the unusual wing-shape and the dark, mottled underside provide it with remarkably effective camouflage when it rests among dead foliage or twigs, especially in winter for its hibernation. Its English and biological names both come from the white mark on the underside which can be taken to resemble either a comma or a letter C.

One of the few butterflies that have been becoming more common, it has spread right across the South of England and Wales, and into the Midlands. Commas favour the edges of woodland, but may well breed in the wild parts of gardens if they have the right foodplants, notably Stinging Nettle, Elm and Hop. The butterflies are fond of tree sap and ripe or rotting fruit as well as flowers.

The female lays eggs singly or in small groups on the upper surface of leaves. When it hatches, the caterpillar moves underneath and its feeding peppers the leaf with small holes. When it is fully grown, its front half is brown, but the rear half of the back is pure white and covered with immaculately white, branched spines. The chrysalis imitates withered leaves in appearance, with a knobbly shape and markings like veins.

The butterflies which emerge from hibernation lay their eggs in April and May. The first eggs to be laid produce butterflies paler than normal, with a light ochreous underside. These, known as form *hutchisoni*, develop quickly and breed again to produce another generation of adults in July and August. The later spring eggs produce the normal form, which emerge only a little ahead of the *hutchisoni* progeny and go into hibernation earlier than this second brood.

Black Bryony
+ web

(coming)

CP.

Comma

The Comma on Black Bryony is a combination you will see in autumn in hedgerows and on the edges of woodlands. Like the Red Admiral and the Small Tortoiseshell, which are around at the same time of year, it is attracted to fruit and to rich colours. The mauvish brown of the background is that of a hedgerow when the weather is damp and a lot of the foliage is dying off – but perhaps my eyes are governed by the colours that I like. I'm fascinated by the structure of cobwebs, which I often use to link a painting together, just as they link flower to flower in the wild. They are something we all remember from our school days – making little hoops of twigs and collecting up cobwebs.   G.B.

Sweet Brier,